BY-GONE BROCK.

IN.

Postal Coi   ...cations

The Brockenhurst Grammar School

The Telephone in Brockenhurst

The Brokenhurst Gas Company

The Brockenhurst Volunteer Fire Brigade

The Morant Hall, later New Forest Hall

The New Forest Lawn Tennis and Croquet Club.

The Brockenhurst Nursing Association.

The Carnival for the C of E School enlargement

D. Topp, *Family Butcher*

ENGLISH MEAT.

Prime Ox Beef.
Wether Mutton.
Home-made Sausages.
Dairy-Fed Pork

Families supplied on Lowest

Brookley Road.

BROCKENHURST

c1900 Advertisement

Postal Communications

In 1817 the Post Office was situated in the Butchers Shop, now being used as the Letting Agency office, next to the Forester's Arms. Later it was situated opposite the Rose & Crown in Lyndhurst Road (nowadays called The Huntsman Inn).

After the railway arrived it moved to the baker's shop, on the corner of Mill Lane run by the Butt family, opposite Ash Cottage. At that time there was only one postal round in the village, this was up to Setley, across to Caters, then to Hinchelsea, down the Weirs through Brookley Lane (Road) and back to the Post Office. Mail for Brokenhurst Manor and Rhinefield had special bags. Other residents outside the postman's route had to collect their mail.

Outgoing mail was taken to Lymington in a two wheeled cart for sorting before it was returned to be put on the mail train. On the way the postman could be handed a letter, together with a penny for the postage.

The telegraph office was at the station, using railway lines.

In c1896 the premises of Pot-Pourri in Brookley Road, were built and this became the village post office; Mr. Joshua Bromfield was postmaster. With the development of the Brookley Manor land a Crown Post Office was built in 1908. The Post Mistress was the widowed Mrs. Broomfield.

The new premises were built with a Post Office counter, a sorting office, a room to accommodate a future telephone exchange and a Post Master's flat. It became the centre to sort incoming and outgoing mail both for that collected and delivered in Brockenhurst, Beaulieu, Lyndhurst, Minstead and Bramshaw.

Mrs. Broomfield and Postal Staff. C1909

The sorting office was extended after the war and was the base of a dozen mail vans. Additionally, a sub-post office was at the Butts Lawn Stores until the 1960's.

The last time for posting at the main office was 10 p.m. weekdays and 9.30 p.m. Sundays. Urgent letters could be posted in the mail box on the midnight mail train.

The Post Office was downgraded to a sub-office and finally closed in its 1908 building in August 2019.

Post Office Directory.

Postmaster, Mr. E. R. WARREN.

Letters arrive weekdays at :— 6 a.m. 10 a.m. 2.45 p.m.

Particulars of Letter Box Collections—Town and Rural.

		Weekdays.				Sundays.
Brockenhurst S.O.		11.15 a.m.	1.15 p.m.	3.15 p.m.	*10 p.m.	9.30 p.m.
Broadlands	...	8.15 a.m.	12.30 p.m.		7.30 p.m.	8 p.m.
New Park ...	...	7 a.m.			4.15 p.m.	
Ober Road	...	8.30 a.m.	12.30 p.m.		7.30 p.m.	7.45 p.m.
Railway Gates	...	8.15 a.m.	1 p.m.		7.15 p.m.	7.35 p.m.
Railway Station	...	8.15 a.m.	1 p.m.		8 p.m.	7.40 p.m.
Setley	...	7.15 a.m.			7 p.m.	7.25 p.m.
Waters Green	...	7.45 a.m.	12.20 p.m.		7.15 p.m.	7.40 p.m.
Weirs	...	8.15 a.m.			7.45 p.m.	7.55 p.m.
Whitley Ridge	...		12.30 p.m.		7.30 p.m.	7.30 p.m.
Wide Lane	...	8.15 a.m.	11 a.m.		6.45 p.m.	7.15 p m.

* Collection on Saturdays at 9 p.m

1929 village collection times. There were three deliveries.

"I am putting you through". The Telephone in Brockenhurst

The present Post Office building was built 1908 and incorporated a room for a manual telephone exchange. On 15th September 1910 the main telegraph pole, that would support the lines bringing calls to the village and route them to subscribers, was erected.

Erecting the first pole.
15th September 1910

The telephone number of properties that were connected in the days of the manual exchange may still have the original number as the last two or three digits of their present number. Richard Purkess' number was 22 and the final number, after 90 years was 622322.

By 1919 there were 50 subscribers and these were listed in a publication by Mr. J. R. Stevens, the local printer. With the publication of the monthly Brockenhurst Bulletin the local directory was regularly updated by the postmaster.

The Bulletin of September 1929 listed 208 subscribers but this number had increased to 250 in 1934.

To relieve the monotony of the exchange operators waiting for calls, Stanley Orchard, who had a workshop at 'Nordons', in Waters Green, would, each morning on arrival, turn on his radio, ring the exchange and place his receiver by the radio so the telephone girls could plug in and enjoy music.

The new automatic exchange was built in 1939 on its present site in Sway Road, when over 400 numbers changed to four digits.

The last telephone directory, with the Brockenhurst exchange name and four-digit numbers, was issued in August 1979, listing over 1,000 subscribers.

In the early 1980's the exchange was enlarged, and all numbers were then listed under the Lymington exchange and increased to five and finally to six digits.

The Post office, Brockenhurst c1914

The Brockenhurst Grammar School

In the last decade of the nineteenth century there were Pupil Teacher centres at Christchurch, Ringwood and Lymington. These establishments gave further education to senior pupils at village schools who could give assistance to the teachers.

In 1909 Hampshire Education Committee decided to amalgamate these centres to form one at Brockenhurst. The first venue used was the school room at the Wesleyan church in Avenue Road.

The Wesleyan School room rear left. C1910

The centre moved to Blandford Lodge in the Rise in 1910 and remained there until 1913 with a roll of 26 pupils.

In 1913 a move was made to Highwood Road, accommodated in newly built wooden classrooms under the Headmistress, Miss Ward. By 1921 the roll had risen to 155 and it was renamed the Brockenhurst County School. During the twenties and early thirties additional buildings were added.

Original County School Buildings in Highwood Road when used as the Village Hall in 1975.

7

Miss Ward died in 1935 and Mr RH May B.Sc., Headmaster of Farnborough Grammar School, was appointed Headmaster from the 1936 summer term.

In 1936 the County Council purchased the present college site and playing fields from the Careys Manor estate. The original plans were to provide a new school for boys here and use the Highwood Road site for a girls' school until a new girls' school was built at New Milton but the war put an end to this and the Highwood Road site was taken over by the Portsmouth Southern Secondary School for Boys from 1939 until 1945.

The school on Lyndhurst Road was completed for occupation in 1939 with a roll of 390 pupils and a change of name to the County High School.

The County High School opened in September 1939

Mr. May retired in 1949 and Dr. Wood was appointed headmaster. The school became a Grammar School. By 1960, there were over 1,100 pupils. In 1973 it became a sixth form college and later Brockenhurst College.

The Brockenhurst Gas Company

On the left side of the Sway Road railway bridge approach was the entrance to the Brockenhurst Gas Company's works.

The manager's house and gas holder

The Trust, originally known as 'Residence for the District Nurse', was changed to 'The Groome Trust' when the cottage was sold on 18th February 1988. The proceeds, are now used to provide support for less well-off families, and some community projects.

The Morant Hall, later New Forest Hall

The Morant Trustees built and managed the Hall and the New Forest Croquet and Lawn Tennis Club (*following article*) which occupied the land where Forest Hall, Sutton Place, Noel Close and Chestnut Road were developed.

The hall was designed by Capt. Cecil Sutton, the Morant's agent, and completed in 1911, and initially was known as the Coronation Hall. The ballroom had a sprung dance floor, alcoves and a stage; 600 people could be seated in it. Attached was a supper room, large enough to accommodate 200 people for a social gathering or meeting, along with appropriate kitchen facilities. A roller-skating floor was provided.

The first function was on King George V's Coronation day, 22nd June 1911, when a free tea was provided for 1,000 members of the community. In the evening a 'Fancy Dress Ball' started at 10 pm with dancing continuing until 3 am, admission 1/6d (7.5p). In April 1912 an entertainment was held to raise money for the Mayor of Southampton's Titanic Disaster Fund, over 500 people attended and £115 was raised.

On the outbreak of war, in August 1914, a committee of local people was formed to organize the furnishing and the supply of equipment required to use the hall as a fifty-bed hospital. The first patients were brought from the Royal Victoria Military Hospital at Netley, in October 1914. Members of the local community arranged entertainment for the patients.

In November 1914 King George V and Queen Mary met British and Belgian soldiers here when they visited the Indian Lady Hardinge hospitals.

J.R. Stevens, the local printer, produced a colour programme of the Christmas Day entertainment in 1914.

The Morant Hall, Lyndhurst Road (then High Road) c1925

The Morant Hall became a 50 bed hospital in 1914 - pictured left.

When the No. 1 New Zealand Hospital was established at Tile Barn Hill, in 1916, the Hospital at the hall became part of it until 1919.

Post War, The London Touring Cinema gave a performance on August 1st 1920. This was a group of ex-servicemen who toured the country, complete with their own generator to produce the current for the projection of films.

The hall was refurbished in 1921 when electric light was installed, provided by a generator. It was the social centre of the area being the venue for every kind of occasion from the Infant Welfare Christmas Party to the most elaborate of Hunt Balls, the local school concerts to entertainment broadcasts by the B.B.C.

Among the regular social charity functions were the annual Bachelors' Ball and the Spinsters' Ball. The annual Railwaymen's Ball, was organised by the railwaymen from Totton to Christchurch for the Woking Railway Staff Children's Orphanage. Special trains were run to take the dancers home. The Bernardo Boys band entertained annually to raise funds for the charity.

The W. I. Christmas party in the hall 1922

Events were run by the Parochial Entertainments Committee to raise funds for the local hospitals, clubs and C of E School, from September until Easter Monday. Often there were over 450 people attending their dances, a popular one being on Boxing Day night.

Many local lads and lassies met their future spouses at the regular Saturday night dances. These were so popular that the railway company ran a late train to Lymington after them.

On Friday, 16th November 1928, the hall was the venue for the inauguration of the village's electricity supply, by the West Hampshire Electricity Company. The 'Switch On' ceremony was performed by Mrs. H. A. Alexander, sister of the late Edward Morant.

Among the regular exhibitions held in the hall were the three-day New Forest Arts and Crafts Exhibition and the area Women's Institute exhibition.

During the Second World War it became the centre for entertainment, not only for the local population, but for the troops and airmen posted around the village.

During the annual 'Savings Week' a full week's programme of films, concerts and dances was held.

On Friday 14th August 1942 the B.B.C. broadcast a live show from the hall, from 10.15 – 10.45 pm. It was a cabaret by Gillie Potter and Jackie Hunter in the interval of a evening's dancing with music provided by Melville Christie and his Dance Orchestra.

Among the concert parties that entertained was one organized by Dr Horace King, a master at the Southampton Taunton's School, at that time evacuated to Bournemouth. Later in his parliamentary career he was Speaker of the House of Commons . On retirement from the Commons he entered the House of Lords taking the title of Lord Maybray-King.

When the Morant Trustees sold most of their property, to the north of the railway on the 25th January 1951, the Morant Hall was among the lots, but was withdrawn when it did not reach the reserve price.

The Hall was later bought by a syndicate in which Capt. Sutton and Mr. Smith, the landlord of the 'Rose & Crown', were interested. Saturday night dances and balls continued until the final sale of the hall. Some events transformed the hall into forest glades, desert islands, etc. to provide an atmosphere.

The name changed to the 'New Forest Hall' on January 1st 1952.

Dancing at the hall c1956

The New Forest Hall with a 'For Sale' sign c1974. The cottage on the left was a village bakery in 1817.

In the autumn, of 1952, the Grammar School was close to securing the property to provide additional accommodation for the school. It was intended to let out the hall during evenings and at weekends and to restore the tennis courts. On the day before the agreement was signed, Mr. Morant cancelled it and negotiations collapsed.

In May 1954 a B.B.C. production of 'Any Questions' was, broadcast from the hall. The question master was Freddie Grisewood and the panel consisted of Sir Robert Boothby M.P., Richard Crossman M.P., Sir Graham Savage and Arthur Street.

'The Optimists' were a group who started performing, in the 1950's. The annual Village Pantomime, originated from a drama group of the Women's Institute and various groups have continued this village tradition. Entrance to the Saturday night dances, in 1954, was 3/- (15p), 8 p.m. to mid-night.

In August 1956 the Brockenhurst Parish Council called an emergency meeting of parishioners to consider an offer by Capt. Sutton M.B.E. to sell the New Forest Hall to the Village for £16,500, for possible use as a community centre. The offer was declined. In 1972 the Hall was again offered to the village, but the asking price was considered too large for locally obtainable funds. It was then sold for development and Sutton Place and Forest Hall houses were built.

The New Forest Lawn Tennis and Croquet Club

On the 11th May 1912, Mrs. Edward Morant performed the opening ceremony of the New Forest Lawn Tennis and Croquet Club on the grounds attached to the Morant Hall. There were six grass tennis courts and three croquet lawns. An open Croquet Tournament was first held on 28th April 1913.

Brockenhurst Tennis Club Members c1912

The first open Lawn Tennis Tournament under Lawn Tennis Association rules, was held on 25th July 1912 when 90 players entered.

From 1912, tennis at Brockenhurst featured in the English Lawn Tennis calendar, being the venue of the Annual New Forest Open Lawn Tennis Tournament attracting 600 entries for the week-long event.

On the Friday night a Tournament Ball was held, followed by a 'Cinderella' dance on the Finals Day, Saturday. Proceeds from these were donated to the Lymington and Lyndhurst Hospitals.

In 1927 three hard tennis courts were added. The eventual number of courts was three hard courts and 12 grass courts.

The Tournament was not held between 1915-18 and was unable to be held in 1919. The refurbishment of the hotels, taken over by the military during the war had not been completed. From 1920 it was held annually until 1939 but was only revived once in 1947. In August a Junior Tennis Tournament was held from 1923-1939 and from 1946-9

In 1933 two members of the Australian Davis Cup team played and were successful in winning singles and doubles matches. A club house with squash and badminton courts was opened in 1934. Inter-county squash championship games were played here.

When the late Queen Elizabeth, the Queen Mother,

The Centre Court c1930

stayed with her uncle, the Hon. Malcolm Bowles-Lyons, at Whitley Ridge, she most likely played tennis here as her uncle was a member.

In 1952 Noel Close and Chestnut Road were developed on this ground.

The Carnival for the C of E School enlargement 1st June 1914

In 1912 the Church of England school had been enlarged at a cost of £1,840, of which £160 remained to be raised. On the initiative of the trades and working men of the village a Carnival committee was formed, chaired by the Rev. Arthur Chambers assisted by Rev. G.C. Williams and Mr. Phillip Russen, as secretaries, to raise this sum.

Huntsmen lead the carnival procession

There was great activity in the village as traders designed and assembled their floats, (15 in all), others designed tableaux (9), decorated prams and cycles, and mums made the Fancy-Dress costumes for themselves and their children. All had to be ready for the Whit Monday Carnival on 1st June 1914. The line-up included:

Trade and Industries Floats: Led by the Burley Brass Band - Grocer, Mr. Purkess; Butcher, Mr. Holtom; Baker Mr. St. John; Milk Cart, Mr. Goater; Butcher, Mr. Dear; Grocer, Plumbly's Stores; The Village Blacksmith, Mr. Street; Rustic Manufacturers, Messer's Lunn Brothers; Old Men Wood Binding, Messer's Lunn Brothers; Boot Repairing, Elliott and Son; Plumbing, Messer's Plumbly Bros; Wheelwright, Mr. F. Collins; Printing, Mr. J. R. Stevens; Building, Mr. H. Russen; Gardening, Mr. G. Place.

Fancy Costumes: preceded by the Cadnam Brass Band included seven mounted and thirty-five walking entries, followed by four Decorated Cycles and Prams.

Tableaux, preceded by the Brockenhurst Brass Band – 'Empire Tableau' by the Misses Russen and Chandler; 'Charcoal Burner taking King Rufus's body to Winchester August 2nd 1100' Mr. R. Purkess; 'The Military Hospital' Mr. G. W. Chalk; 'Foresters' Court "Morant"; 'Cowboys and Indians' arranged by Miss N. Bartlett: 'Gipsy Camp' Mr. Chamberlain; 'Fairy Tableaux' arranged by Miss E. Purkess; 'Long Eared Ponies' Miss Minty; 'Strolling Musicians' Messer H. Smith and E. Jenvey, Mrs. Fairbrother, and Misses B. Jenvey and Churchill; 'Weary Willie and Tiered Tim in Donkey Cart' Messers Smith and W. Dukes; Decorated cart, Sir Berkley Pigott.

School children in costume and Alexander's Ragtime Band conducted by Mr. Langham and the Rev. Arthur Chambers.

The Carnival procession at Balmer Lawn

Richard Purkess, Grocer

Mr H. Russen, Builder

Richard Purkess, Baker

2nd cart entered!

The Carnival route started at the school, in Wide Lane (Sway Road) and pro-ceeded along The Grove (The Rise), along Ober Farm Road (Rhinefield Road) turning around the circle at the Forest Park Hotel, then back to the road that was later named Meerut Road, to the main road and left to Balmer Lawn where the procession turned to go up towards the railway gates. Before the gates it turned down Brookley Lane (Road) to the bank corner where it turned left into Wide Lane and then again went down The Grove, turned right to come up through the village shops and on up to the level crossing to Mill Lane and the fete in the field inside the Lodge at Brockenhurst Park.

Reverend Arthur Chambers on his tricycle

Purkess The Charcoal Burner

At the Carnival ground there was a Pig guessing competition (*details have been lost but the author presumes the weight or name)*, tug-of-war, Quoits match, Maypole Dancing and sports with a fair ground atmosphere with a roundabout, shooting gallery and other attractions. Bands played throughout the afternoon and evening, and the Fete was brought to an enjoyable close with dancing.

Total receipts of the Carnival amounted to a handsome sum of £121/1/8d.